ON GENOCIDE

ON GENOCIDE

BY JEAN-PAUL SARTRE

*and a summary of the evidence
and the judgments of the
International War Crimes Tribunal
by Arlette El Kaïm-Sartre*

BEACON PRESS   BOSTON

Contents

A Summary of the Evidence and the Judgments:
An Introduction

BY ARLETTE EL KAÏM-SARTRE

ON NOVEMBER 13, 1966 in response to Bertrand Russell's appeal, personalities of varied political convictions from different countries met in London and decided to form an International War Crimes Tribunal. In a statement adopted on November 16 at the close of these preliminary meetings the founding members described the reasons which led them to form this Tribunal:

Every day the world press and especially the American press relates facts which, if proved, would represent multiple violations of principles established by the Nuremberg Tribunal and rules fixed by international conventions. Disturbed and indignant over the suffering endured by the Vietnamese people and convinced that humanity must know the truth in order to pass serious and impartial judgment on the events which take place in Vietnam and determine those responsible for these acts, we have agreed to meet at the invitation of Lord Bertrand Russell to scrupu-

3

lously examine these facts and to compare them with the guiding principles of law which govern them.

Although we have been invested in our duties by no official organization, we have accepted this responsibility in the interest of humanity and for the protection of civilization. We act of our own free will, independent of all governments or all official or semi-official organizations and with the firm conviction that we express the profound anguish and remorse felt by a great number of our fellow men in many countries. We are convinced that we will help awaken the conscience of the people.

We thus consider ourselves as a Tribunal which, even if powerless to impose sanctions, will have to answer the following questions:

1) Has the government of the United States (and the governments of Australia, New Zealand and South Korea) committed aggression in the sense of international law?

2) Has the American Army used or experimented with new weapons prohibited by the laws of war (gas, special chemicals, etc.)?

3) Have there been, and if so on what scale, intentional bombings of purely civilian installations, namely of hospitals, schools, sanatoriums, dams, etc.?

4) Are Vietnamese prisoners subjected to inhumane treatment forbidden by the

laws of war, including torture or mutilation?

5) Have there been unjustifiable reprisals against the civilian population, namely the execution of hostages? Has there been creation of hard-labor camps, deportation of the population or other acts tending towards the extermination of the population which can legally be called acts of genocide?

If the Tribunal finds that one or all of these crimes have been committed, it will be up to its members to determine who bears the responsibility.

Our Tribunal will examine all evidence submitted, from whatever source it may come. No qualified witness desiring to testify about events relative to our inquiry will be refused the opportunity to do so. The South Vietnamese Liberation Front and the government of the Democratic Republic of Vietnam have assured us that they are ready to cooperate with us, to furnish necessary information and to help us verify the exactitude and merits of this information. Prince Sihanouk, the chief of state of Cambodia, has offered to help us gather evidence as well. We firmly believe that they will honor their promises and we gratefully accept their help without however giving up our own points of view nor our own principles. As a Tribunal, we renew the appeal that Lord Bertrand Russell addressed to the United States Government in his own name. We ask the United States Government to submit or to have submitted any useful evidence and to instruct its civil servants and representatives to appear before us to support their point of view.

Without fear of anyone nor under cover of anyone, our goal is to establish the truth about this war. We sincerely hope that our efforts will contribute to justice in the world, the restoration of peace and the liberation of oppressed peoples.

The first session of the Russell Tribunal was held in Stockholm from May 2 to 10, 1967. It set itself the task of answering the first and third questions: those on aggression and civilian bombings. In his inaugural speech Jean-Paul Sartre, the executive president of the Tribunal, specified that the Tribunal would judge the crimes committed in Vietnam by the definitions and standards of existing international law, and particularly the judgments of the Nuremberg Tribunal which judged German war crimes in 1945.

Aggression

The Nuremberg Tribunal defined *crimes against peace* as follows:

planning, preparation, initiation or waging of a war of aggression, or a war in violation of international treaties, agreements or assurances, or participation in a common plan or conspiracy for the accomplishment of any of the foregoing [war crimes] (Article 6 (a) of the Charter of the International Military Tribunal).

Moreover, Article 2, section 4, of the United Nations Charter stipulates:

> All Members shall refrain in their international relations from the threat or use of force against the territorial integrity or political independence of any state, or in any other manner inconsistent with the Purposes of the United Nations.

The various historians who examined American policy towards Vietnam for the Tribunal agreed, in the light of the facts, that the United States began to be interested in Vietnam at the end of the Second World War and its policy began to be unquestionably aggressive from 1950 onwards.

The war has not in fact been the result of a chain of events for which no one is responsible. The United States had — and still has — a purpose: to maintain in the capitalist sphere a country not recognized at Yalta as a zone of Soviet influence, and to contain, according to the domino theory, revolution in Asia within the borders of China. It was to accomplish this purpose that the United States granted France massive aid for the pursuit of the war in Indochina ($1,450 million from 1950 up to the signing of the Geneva Accords). It was necessary, at any price, to check an eventual socialist revolution in Vietnam. Because of the fear that the Vietnamese people, once free, would choose communism, they had to be prevented from winning.

When finally victorious over the French after Dien Bien Phu, the Vietnamese people prepared to choose their own future according to their right to independence and unity which the Geneva Accords of 1954 expressly recognized. The United States then endeavored by other means to deprive them of this right, which moreover the United Nations Charter recognizes as that of all people (Article 1, section 2).

The United States didn't sign the Geneva Accords; however, by the unilateral declaration of its delegate, Ambassador Walter Bedell Smith, at the close of the conference, the United States government pledged to respect them in abstaining "from the threat or the use of force in order to disturb them, in accordance with Article 2, section 4, of the Charter of the United Nations . . ." However, several days beforehand, while the Geneva Conference was still in session, the United States had forced Ngo Dinh Diem as prime minister upon the Emperor Bao Dai. Henceforward, through Diem and through the different "governments" which followed the deposing of Bao Dai, the Americans had a grasp on South Vietnam. But for American influence to continue, none of the principal clauses of the Accords could be respected because they would lead the people of Vietnam towards their real independence.

What in fact did the Accords provide for? First, to facilitate the suspension of hostilities, a demarcation line between the North and the South of Vietnam — but *provisional* and intended only to permit the separation and withdrawal of the forces of the two parties (Article 1 of the Agreement on Cessation of Hostilities). "The military demarcation line is a provisional line and should not in any way be interpreted as constituting a political or a territorial boundary," again specified the final declaration of the Geneva Conference. Next, an essential clause of the Accords provided for general elections, in the North as well as in the South in July, 1956, which would permit the reunification of the country:

> The Conference declares that, so far as Vietnam is concerned, the settlement of political problems, effected on the basis of respect for the principles of independence, unity and territorial integrity, shall permit Vietnamese people to enjoy the fundamental freedoms, guaranteed by democratic institutions established as a result of free general elections by secret ballot. In order to ensure that sufficient progress in the restoration of peace has been made, and that all the necessary conditions obtain for free expression of the national will, general elections shall be held in July, 1956, under the supervision of an international

commission composed of representatives of the Member States of the International Supervisory Commission, referred to in the agreement on the cessation of hostilities. Consultations will be held on this subject between the competent representative authorities of the two zones from 20 July, 1955, onwards (Paragraph 7, Final Declaration of the Geneva Conference).

The Accords also prohibited the "introduction into Vietnam of any reinforcements in the form of all types of arms, munitions and other war material, such as combat aircraft, naval craft, pieces of ordnance, jet engines and jet weapons, and armored vehicles . . ." (Article 17 (a) of the Agreement on Cessation of Hostilities). It was also provided that "Each party undertakes to refrain from any reprisals or discrimination against persons or organizations on account of their activities during the hostilities and to guarantee their democratic liberties" (Article 14 (c) of the Agreement on Cessation of Hostilities).

In its judgment the International War Crimes Tribunal accuses the United States of having violated the Geneva Accords in four essential points:

1) The Americans implanted themselves militarily in South Vietnam. From 1955 onwards, under pretext of an "economic" agreement, the United States reinforced the military potential of the Diem government; consequently an American military command

10

and enormous military forces were placed in South Vietnam contrary to the provisions for military withdrawal in the Accords.

2) The Accords barely signed, they sought after former resistants to French colonialism, by means of the South Vietnamese government which they controlled, and inflicted large-scale reprisals against these resistants in spite of the ban which the Accords stipulated.

3) and 4) In considering the demarcation line between the two zones as a definite political boundary and preventing elections, they constituted the South of Vietnam as a separate state.

Eisenhower admits in *Mandate for Change:*

I have never talked or corresponded with a person knowledgeable in Indochinese affairs who did not agree that had elections been held . . . possibly 80% of the population would have voted for the Communist Ho Chi Minh as their leader rather than Bao Dai.

The United States was determined that this result should not occur — in contempt of the right of the people and of its own commitments, with no other justification but the necessities of its policy. That is why the Saigon government, chosen by the Americans, and depending entirely upon them economically as well as militarily, refused the elections. When American officials pretend that the purpose of United States action is to safeguard

11

the "independence of South Vietnam," they are in contradiction with the Geneva Accords, according to which, the seventeenth parallel being only a temporary line, the entire Vietnamese people should choose its own destiny. The International War Crimes Tribunal thus concluded: "The responsibility for the passage to a state of war falls upon the United States of America."

But these violations, this brutal interference in the affairs of a people were not enough to assure the United States of complete domination over Vietnam. From 1954 to 1959 the Vietnamese people, confident in the Geneva Accords, had waged an exclusively political struggle for their application. When a terrible repression swept down upon those who dared claim this right to independence which had been granted them before the world, they went over to armed struggle which the National Liberation Front has been directing since 1960. This struggle, legitimately undertaken and supported by the people, could not be handled by American troops, and so the United States intensified its aggression after 1964 by massive bombings in the North.

The Russell Tribunal has examined official American documents which try to justify American intervention in the North, in particular the legal memorandum entitled "The Legality of United States Participation in the Defense of Vietnam," presented in the Senate Foreign Affairs Committee on March 4, 1966. The essential argument is that the South has been the victim of an "armed attack" by the North. This armed attack is represented by the infiltration of armed and unarmed men from the North to the South. The Tribunal, comparing official American sources, confirmed that they were contradictory.* However, in admitting the highest figures given by American sources, about twenty thousand men are said to have gone from the North to the South from 1959 to 1964. The second White Paper published by the State Department recognizes that ninety thousand men from the South had gone to the North after the Geneva Accords and that the majority of the northern soldiers captured in the South were born in the South. They had hoped to return to their homes after the elections and the reunification of the country. The Geneva Accords had been violated and their hopes shattered. What could be more legitimate than to go home anyway — in arms to take up the struggle, or unarmed? In fact, no American argument could get out of this dilemma: either the Geneva Accords had to be respected and the reunification of the country had to be effected under the responsibility of the signatories without the Americans having anything to do with it, or if the Americans did not consider the Accords valid, then it was perfectly legitimate for

*The memorandum and the second State Department White Paper do not indicate the same figures.

the Vietnamese people, in the North as well as in the South, to take up arms again.

In its judgment the Russell Tribunal categorically rejected the argument of northern aggression against the South, even if infiltrations had been or were becoming more numerous: "In law, it is scarcely necessary to recall that Vietnam constitutes a single and unique nation, and one sees with difficulty how she could aggress against herself." The Tribunal thus concluded:

It follows from the preceding evidence that the United States holds the responsibility for the use of force in Vietnam and that it has *consequently committed against this country a crime of aggression, a crime against peace.*

They have thus violated the provisions of international law forbidding the use of force in international relations, namely the 1928 Paris Pact, called the Kellogg-Briand Pact, of which they were the instigators, and the Charter of the United Nations (Article 2, paragraph 4). This violation of general principles has been accompanied by violations of the particular accords relative to the territory in question, Vietnam, i.e., the Geneva Accords of 1954.

In so doing the United States has unquestionably committed a crime against peace in the sense of Article 6 of the Statute of Nuremberg, a clause accepted by international jurisprudence (Judgments of Nuremberg and Tokyo) and recognized as international law obligatory for all by unanimous resolution of the United Nations on December 11, 1946.

The United States has moreover committed a *crime against the fundamental rights* of the Vietnamese people.

There is reason to add that states such as South Korea, Australia and New Zealand which have in one form or another furnished any aid to American aggression have made themselves accomplices.*

Civilian Bombings

The press informs us every day that Americans bomb Vietnam. But from the reports of Boards of Inquiry that the Russell Tribunal had designated and from eyewitnesses and victims of the bombings, who had come of their own accord to testify, the Tribunal became convinced by degrees that numerous civilians are killed, that these bombings particularly over North Vietnam are massive and most of the time deliberately directed against objectives which are not at all military and are in fact intended to break the morale of the population.

The Boards of Inquiry compared the facts officially presented by the Democratic Republic of Vietnam and the findings made on the scene by

*During the second session, the Russell Tribunal completed its judgment and also condemned the Philippines, Thailand and Japan as accomplices to American aggression in Vietnam.

their own members. These comparisons were numerous: for example, of ninety-five medical institutions reported destroyed by the Vietnamese commissions, thirty-four (thirty-six per cent) were visited by the Boards of Inquiry of the Tribunal. The finding of these boards is that the United States systematically attacks a large number of cities, villages, cooperatives and buildings of a completely civilian nature.

RESULTS OF THESE ATTACKS

1) Against dikes and hydraulic structures: between March and December, 1965, more than 500 aerial attacks. From February to September, 1966, more than one thousand raids. The Boards reported that these attacks were undoubtedly directed against these structures and not against some nearby military objective. One of the boards was present at the bombing of a dike on the River Ma, province of Thanh Hoa. This dike is situated in an isolated and mountainous region, far from any city, road or bridge which could have been considered a military objective. The tribunal has drawn attention in its conclusions to the serious danger of famine that the civilian population risks as a result of the attempts by American forces to destroy these structures.

2) Against hospitals and various medical institutions: ninety-five institutions destroyed in the month of February, 1967. These insti-

tutions are recognizable; the most striking example is that of the Quinh Lap leper colony whose location, a small plain surrounded by mountains, was perfectly isolated for obvious reasons. A Board of Inquiry from the tribunal which visited the ruins verified that this isolation was total. Inaugurated in 1960, visited by several foreign delegations and known by the World Health Organization, it was a pilot center for treatment and research in leprosy. It was thus known throughout the world and there can be no doubt as to its goal and its location. Moreover it was not a hospital but a *little city* where lepers were not only treated but also had a social and cultural life and worked the surrounding land. The details of the attacks undergone by the one hundred sixty buildings of the leper colony until completely destroyed are worth telling because they obviously prove the will to destroy *precisely* this leper colony and to *kill the greatest possible number of people.*

The first attack took place on June 12, 1965, by means of explosive bombs and rockets. It did only material damage. The authorities of the leper colony *thought it was a mistake.* The red cross on top of the hospital and especially the knowledge of the purpose of this place were sufficient, it seemed to them, for an attack not to be deliberately repeated. But the next day a more violent air raid caused one hundred twenty deaths and wounded more than one thousand. The last waves of planes machine-gunned lepers who fled in all directions. After this attack the patients were evacuated to grottoes situated several kilometers away at the foot of some rocky hills, and still isolated. The following attack was directed against these grottoes: the pilots spotted the evacuated lepers; there were thirty-four dead and thirty wounded. Twenty-six other attacks finished off the one hundred sixty buildings. The leper colony is one hundred per cent destroyed.

3) Against educational institutions: it is not only a question of schools destroyed during the bombing of a city but also of village schools. One should know that, in the latter case, the school is the only building of durable construction, which makes it perfectly recognizable amidst the surrounding straw huts. Three hundred ninety-one schools were destroyed from August 5, 1964, to March, 1967. The majority of those that the Boards of Inquiry visited were situated far from any military objective. Schoolchildren were killed; pilots are known to have machine-gunned children who fled.

4) Against religious institutions: eighty churches and thirty pagodas have been attacked or destroyed. Numerous priests, bonzes and churchgoers have been killed: seventy-two dead in the church of Kien Trung (near Phat Diem) alone, attacked on April 24, 1966, during the vesper hour.

5) Against populous places and industrial districts: whole cities and villages, of which there are many agricultural cooperatives and

food production plants underwent intensive bombings without military objectives being near. The city of Thanh Hoa for example, was subjected to seventy attacks up to March, 1967, and had to be almost entirely evacuated. The nearest military objective is the bridge at Ham Rong, eight kilometers away as the crow flies.

Before the Second World War broke out, a certain number of attempts were made to elaborate a code of aerial warfare. The 1923 Convention of The Hague authorized the "bombing of military forces, and military establishments engaged in war production" but proscribed "aerial bombings destined to terrorize the population." The Charter of the Military Tribunal of Nuremberg considers as war crimes ". . . the wanton destruction of cities, towns and villages or devastation not justified by military necessity."

And the fourth Geneva Convention of August 12, 1949, stipulates that "Civilian hospitals organized to give care to the wounded and sick, the infirm and maternity cases, may in no circumstances be the object of attack, but shall at all times be respected and protected by the Parties to the conflict." (Article 18).

The International War Crimes Tribunal considers that the United States cannot ignore treaties to which it has been party when the American Constitution declares: "This Constitution, and the

Laws of the United States which shall be made in Pursuance thereof, and all Treaties made or which shall be made, under the Authority of the United States, shall be the supreme Law of the land . . ." (Constitution of the United States of America, Article VI, clause 2).

WORSENING CIRCUMSTANCES

The Russell Tribunal has concluded that American troops do not bomb non-military objectives by chance, without worry about the fate of the population, but with knowledge and the intention of killing more and more civilians. This intention is clear if one knows that air raids are always preceded by reconnaissance flights, the modern technology of the weapons used results in great accuracy and that the planes repeatedly return to the same objectives. It becomes unquestionable when one knows that the United States uses widely a kind of bomb recently perfected which has been especially designed to strike a defenseless population: market crowds, straw-hut villages, populous districts of cities, etc. These antipersonnel bombs, called steel pellet bombs or cluster bomb units, have no effect, indeed, on concrete or steel. Their existence has been reported since June, 1966, by the American press, but the United States government officially disclosed their use in Vietnam only in May, 1967, several days after the close of the first session of the Russell Tribunal.

These weapons cause considerable mortality. Each bomb contains three hundred to four hundred smaller bombs (two types — pineapple or guava); inside each of the latter there are numerous steel pellets (about three hundred) from five to six millimeters in diameter. The mother bomb explodes either by touching the ground or by striking a branch or a wall. It frees more than one hundred thousand pellets, each of which can cause a fatal wound. If, indeed, they cannot penetrate a wall nor reach military personnel protected only by sandbags, their penetration power in the human body, on the other hand, is very great. The same individual may be struck by several fragments; each of them must be removed surgically. As the trajectory of these tiny projectiles is long and irregular inside the body, the lesions caused by one fragment alone are numerous, varied, difficult to detect and require delicate operations. The failure of the surgeon to recognize one of the lesions can be fatal. Sometimes the projectile cannot be removed; there are many victims who will suffer all their life from serious troubles related to this foreign body in the organism, such as the young schoolteacher who testified before the Tribunal, whose brain had been injured in the bombing of her school.

Along with the fragmentation bombs, during

the same raids American aircraft dropped napalm and phosphorus so that fires retarded first aid. Many attacks took place on sleeping cities in the middle of the night. Can there be any doubt that this was done with the intention of accomplishing a greater massacre? Were it not for the excellence of civilian defense and the evacuation of certain cities, the United States would be responsible for hundreds of thousands of additional deaths.

The International War Crimes Tribunal thus concluded:

> . . . that in subjecting a civilian population and civilian objectives of the Democratic Republic of Vietnam to intensive and systematic bombing, the United States has committed *a war crime*.
>
> Beyond the condemnation of this crime as a whole, the Tribunal is firm in stating that fragmentation bombs of type CBU, whose only reason for existence is to strike the civilian population at a maximum, must be considered as weapons forbidden by the laws and practices of war.
>
> Confronted with the resistance of a people which intends to peacefully and freely exercise its right to complete independence and territorial integrity (United Nations resolution of December 14, 1960), the United States Government has given these war crimes, by their extensiveness and their frequency, the character of crimes against

humanity (Article 6 of the Charter of Nuremberg).

These crimes cannot merely be considered as the consequences of a war of aggression of which they condition the pursuit.

Because of their systematic use in order to check the fundamental rights of the Vietnamese people, their unity and will for peace, the crimes against humanity of which the United States Government has rendered itself guilty become a fundamental element of the crime of aggression, supreme crime including all the others, according to the terms of the sentence of Nuremberg.

The second session of the International War Crimes Tribunal was held in Roskilde, Denmark, from November 20 to December 1, 1967. It was to pronounce judgment on the use of weapons prohibited by the laws of war and on the treatment of prisoners and the civilian population by the American Army; lastly it was to decide if the whole of the conduct of the war by the American government and American troops could legally be classified as genocide.

The Tribunal had renewed its appeal to the United States government to send a qualified and authorized representative capable of answering accusations brought against it. In vain. The Tribunal heard spontaneous testimony of persons returned from Vietnam and experts' reports in addition to delegations from the Democratic Republic of Vietnam and the National Liberation Front, Vietnamese victims, the reports of a commission that it had sent to South Vietnam and that of a commission sent to the United States which presented, among others, three Americans who had come to testify before the Tribunal — two young men who had just finished their military service, Peter Martinsen and David Tuck, and Donald Duncan, a former Special Forces officer and former instructor at Fort Bragg.

Illegal Weapons

We have already described fragmentation bombs: these are weapons of massive destruction contrary to the principle of immunity of the civilian population and at the same time weapons equipped to cause useless suffering which is contrary to the 1907 Convention of The Hague, Article 23.

The American government is responsible for the use of other prohibited and just as deadly weapons, in particular gases and chemicals called defoliants. The scientific commission of the Tribunal established the use of the following gases: CN, DM, CN–DM, CS, either in the open air for the attack of a given zone or inside shelters, hiding places and tunnels to drive out enemy elements. These shelters are in fact often used by the civilian population for protection against aerial attacks or

24

to escape, after the destruction of villages, from regroupment camps or interrogations.

The Tribunal investigated the question of whether these gases were capable of having lethal effects. Statements by American officials present them as temporarily incapacitating, non-dangerous products constituting "a humane method of cleaning out an enemy zone where there are women and children" (according to an official spokesman of the American command on March 22, 1965). However, the reports of Vietnamese authorities, supported by precise dates and places, show hundreds of dead.

The scientific commission conducted experiments on animals with samples gathered on the scene. One of them was done with DM. A concentration of fifteen milligrams per liter caused the death of a monkey in forty-five minutes — remember that a DM grenade contains two hundred grams of the chemical. Another experiment was done with CS. Subjected to a concentration of five milligrams per liter, a monkey died in twenty-five minutes. Even if one admits that the people affected are in the open or can escape before the concentration of gas becomes fatal, the liver and kidney lesions which one or the other provoke are often irremediable. A film made by the Board of Inquiry with extracts of cinema and television newsreels shows the results of spreading these gases in shelters: soldiers pulling out heaps of bodies, principally of women and children who had taken refuge there. Peter Martinsen testified that he had seen about ten young girls seriously poisoned (one of whom, about age fifteen, died several hours later) come out of a tunnel into which tear gas had been sprayed.

The Tribunal thus accepted the conclusions of its scientific commission: toxic gases have been and are still being used in Vietnam; the use of the gases CN, CS and DM is repeated and massive and under such conditions that they become fatal gases. They are therefore combat gases which come under the law of prohibitions of international order.

But what are the conventions which forbid this use? The 1925 Geneva Protocol for "the prohibition of the use in war of asphyxiating, poisonous or other gases" is explicit:

> The undersigned Plenipotentiaries, in the name of their respective Governments:
>
> Whereas the use in war of asphyxiating, poisonous or other gases, and of all analogous liquids, materials or devices, has been justly condemned by the general opinion of the civilised world; and
>
> Whereas the prohibition of such use has been declared in Treaties to which the majority of Powers of the world are Parties; and
>
> To the end that this prohibition shall be universally accepted as a part of International

Law, binding alike the conscience and the practice of nations;

Declare:
That the High Contracting Parties, so far as they are not already Parties to Treaties prohibiting such use, accept this prohibition, agree to extend this prohibition to the use of bacteriological methods of warfare and agree to be bound as between themselves according to the terms of this declaration.

The High Contracting Parties will exert every effort to induce other States to accede to the present Protocol. . . .

At this reference to conventional international law the State Department objected (April 5, 1965) that "the United States Senate never ratified the Geneva Protocol of 1925" and that thus "the United States of America is not bound by this protocol."

The International War Crimes Tribunal did not consider this response significant because the principles of immunity of the civilian population, the prohibition of the use of poison, and the prohibition of weapons adapted to cause useless suffering are rules of common law mentioned in the Hague Conventions of 1907 to which the United States is a signatory and are taken up in war manuals including the 1956 American manual "The Law of Land Warfare," which states:

Force of Treaties Under the Constitution. Under the Constitution of the United States, treaties constitute part of the "supreme Law of the Land" (Art. VI, clause 2). In consequence, treaties relating to the law of war have a force equal to that of laws enacted by the Congress. Their provisions must be observed by both military and civilian personnel with the same strict regard for both the letter and spirit of the law which is required with respect to the Constitution and statutes enacted in pursuance thereof.

Force of Customary Law. The unwritten or customary law of war is binding upon all nations. It will be strictly observed by United States forces, subject only to such exceptions as shall have been directed by competent authority by way of legitimate reprisals for illegal conduct of the enemy. . . . The customary law of war is part of the law of the United States and, insofar as it is not inconsistent with any treaty to which this country is a party or with a controlling executive or legislative act, is binding upon the United States, citizens of the United States, and other persons serving this country (Chapter 1, section I, paragraph 7, clauses b and c).

In addition, on December 5, 1966, the United States and ninety other members of the United Nations passed a resolution in the General Assembly which stated:

The General Assembly,

Guided by the principles of the United Nations Charter and of international law,

Considering that weapons with a massive power of destruction constitute a danger to the whole of mankind and are incompatible with the recognized norms of civilization,

Affirming that it is desirable, in order to safeguard these norms of civilization, to strictly observe the rules of international law on warfare,

Recalling that the Geneva Protocol concerning the prohibition of the use in war of asphyxiating, poisonous and other gases and of bacteriological devices, dated June 17, 1925, was signed and is recognized by many states,

Noting that the Conference of the Committee of the 18 Powers on disarmament has the task of seeking an agreement to stop the development and production of chemical and bacteriological weapons with massive powers of destruction, and the elimination of all these weapons from national arsenals, as advocated in the preliminary proposals of general and complete disarmament which is at present before the Conference.

1. Invites all states to strictly conform to the principles and objectives of the Protocol concerning the prohibition of the use in war of asphyxiating, poisonous or other gases and bacteriological devices, signed in Geneva on June 17, 1925, and condemns any act contrary to these objectives.

2. Invites all states to adhere to the Geneva Protocol of June 17, 1925.

As for defoliants, their use is admittedly intended to drive the enemy out of the forests and to prevent the supplying of rice to the "Vietcong." The scientific commission of the Tribunal challenges the propriety of these means and observes that the results surpass by a wide measure the stated goals. Indeed the substances utilized cannot be simple defoliants for the good reason that no one has yet succeeded in making products which would only cause leaves to fall without damaging the rest of the plant and interrupting the cycle of vegetation. Their massive use in fact destroys thousands of hectares (1 hectare = 2.47 acres) of forests and a large quantity of food crops. As for the second admitted purpose: "starving the Vietcong," can only be attained by also starving and poisoning an important part of the civilian population which lives in Vietcong territory.

The American war manual "The Law of Land Warfare" states: "The foregoing rule does not prohibit measures being taken to dry up springs, to divert rivers and aqueducts from their courses, or to destroy through chemical or bacterial agents harmless to man, crops intended *solely* for consumption by the armed forces (if that fact can be established)."

In the first place, defoliants are harmful to man. To be convinced of it, consider the precautions recommended when these products are used as weed killers in agriculture, for example. The statistics of the National Liberation Front show hundreds of poisonings of which a large number are fatal. Witnesses heard by the Tribunal, whose testimony is part of the dossiers of the Tribunal, confirm these statements. Moreover, there are no crops exclusively intended for the National Liberation Front. A Tribunal commission made inquiries in territory controlled by the National Liberation Front, particularly in the province of Tay Ninh which is the operations zone where in February and March, 1967, the United States staff launched Operation "Junction City." All the rice paddies in this province were poisoned at the same time as all the villages and hamlets were completely destroyed. Part of the population escaped the bombings and the regroupment camps and hid in the forest where they live in miserable straw huts camouflaged in the brush, for this zone has been declared a "cleared zone" or a "free fire zone" and everything that moves is shot upon. To insure their subsistence the peasants are obliged to cultivate minuscle rice paddies at the edge of the forests at night. When spotted by American aircraft, the paddies are automatically destroyed by chemicals dropped by air. The Board of Inquiry saw these barrels of "defoliants" which were thrown into the water of the rice paddies, then peppered with machine-gun fire so that the chemical spread around and poisoned all the plants. The commission is a witness that women and children live there.

The use of so-called defoliants, and the use of gases, do not respect the immunity of the civilian population nor the prohibition against toxic products and equipment inflicting useless suffering, principles contained in the above-mentioned conventions.

The Tribunal equally condemns the use of napalm and phosphorus bombs against the civilian population. The commissions sent to the Democratic Republic of Vietnam as well as to South Vietnam saw entire villages burned by such bombs; numerous wounded were examined on the scene in various hospitals or heard during the two sessions, notably a nine-year-old child hit in a field far from any military objective while he was looking after his buffaloes. These chemicals are extremely deadly for they burn everything within a range of eighty meters around the bomb; they inflict unheard-of suffering; phosphorus in particular continues to burn in the skin for many days and the organism in absorbing it undergoes poisoning which damages the liver. Under the conditions of this war it is impossible to save the seriously wounded for whom skin grafts done by specialized personnel with modern equipment are necessary. Scar formation is slow, and there is formation of *cheloids* which necessitates further operations; the scars remain fragile. Napalm and phosphorus victims thus often remain invalids for life.

The Treatment of Prisoners and the Civilian Population

PRISONERS OF WAR

The United States has never declared war on Vietnam. No one, however, will contend that American troops are not waging a war in Vietnam which brings into play a never before equalled military power. Captured soldiers of the National Liberation Army as well as members of the organized resistance that the Americans call "the Vietcong" and the soldiers of the North Vietnamese Army are thus prisoners of war according to the definition of Article 4 of the third Geneva Convention of 1949. Moreover the 1949 Conventions specify that they are applicable even in the case of undeclared war. These four Conventions deal respectively with the wounded and sick of the armies, wounded and sick shipwrecked at sea, prisoners of war and the protection of civilians. They were ratified by the United States; they are moreover the expression of customary international law and "the principles of the law of nations, as they result from the usages established among civilized peoples, from the laws of humanity and the dictates of the public conscience" (Article 158, fourth Convention).

The third Convention provides several essential obligations for the power which holds the prisoners:

1. The satisfaction of needs called primary needs (Articles 13 and 15):
   — respect of bodily integrity, i.e., prohibiting of mutilation, torture and ill treatment
   — right to elementary care of the person (attendance and food)
2. Respect of the dignity of the person:
   — prohibition of any physical or moral constraint in order to obtain information or collaboration (Article 17)
   — respect of personal effects, furnishing of a decent lodging (Articles 18 and 22)
   — transfer outside of combat zones in satisfactory conditions of health and security (Article 19)
   — regulation of penal and disciplinary sanctions protecting prisoners against any arbitrary decision and insuring rights and means of defense (Articles 82ff.)
   — prohibiting of humiliating treatment, specifically: "Prisoners of war are entitled in all circumstances to respect for their person and their honour. Women shall be treated with all the regard due to their sex." (Article 14)
   — minimal regulation of the prisoners' work (Articles 49 to 57)

— the right to correspond (Articles 69, 73 etc.)

The United States cannot escape these obligations because of the fact that they very often deliver their prisoners to the Saigon government forces; they remain responsible for them in any case because this transfer is illegal: "Prisoners of war may only be transferred by the Detaining Power to a power which is a party to the Convention and after the Detaining Power has satisfied itself of the willingness and ability of such transferee Power to apply the Convention" (Article 12).

Testimony has proved that the United States has not even respected the most imperative of these obligations, that is the respect of bodily integrity of the prisoner and his right to elementary care of his person: torture by water, electricity and bamboo under the nails has been practiced and elementary care has been refused, even to the wounded, before interrogation. Peter Martinsen, who was in the 541st Military Intelligence Detachment and had the job of interrogating prisoners, admitted to having brutalized all the prisoners submitted to him and having tortured those suspected of not telling the truth, not on his own initiative, but because it was the rule. The witness, who served in Vietnam from September, 1966, to June, 1967, thus describes one of the first interrogations which he conducted himself, soon after his arrival in Vietnam:

> . . . We received a group of prisoners — eight or nine, I don't remember exactly. I interrogated one, and I had no data on what kind of work he was doing. He was just presented to me. I started to question him and he kept saying that he was not a Vietcong, that he did not know where the Vietcong was, etc. I was quite sure that he was lying. I was not certain that he belonged to the Vietcong, but I was quite sure he was lying about not knowing where they were. I decided to beat him. This did not help. I struck him with my hand. This did not produce anything except a long string of "I don't know's" and then — as was often the case — another interrogator took my place, an interrogation officer. I told the officer, a lieutenant, that I couldn't get anything out of the prisoner. The lieutenant proceeded to do the same thing that I had been doing, finally beating the prisoner, and this did not work. The lieutenant had an army field telephone which works on batteries and a generator. . . . The interrogation continued with the prisoner being tortured by using the field telephone. The telephones were first secured to his hands and then the field telephone wires were placed on his sexual organs. I left. I could not watch it.

Peter Martinsen witnessed the death of a Vietnamese prisoner after torture by an American captain. He stated, "If I were thoroughly questioned for a long time, I could speak of hundreds of cases of torture." And again: "It is foolishness and lies to say that only the Vietnamese torture. I never saw an interrogation conducted by Vietnamese; I don't know what they do when they interrogate. I assume they do exactly what we do, but I don't think they have any compunctions about leaving scars."

When the tribunal asked him if high-ranking officers knew about the tortures, Peter Martinsen answered, "Lieutenant colonels know about it. . . . Occasionally they witnessed interrogations in which beatings occurred."

Contrary to the stipulations of the Third Geneva Convention the American Army gives prisoners to South Vietnamese troops — confirms the same witness — knowing full well the treatment they will undergo. Still contrary to the stipulations of this Convention, American troops deliberately leave seriously wounded prisoners without care. The same witness tells:

There were some people in a tunnel and the Americans found the tunnel entrance. They looked inside the tunnel and found it was occupied. They immediately gassed it with tear gas. It might have been "anti-riot" gas. Then they proceeded to chase the people from the tunnel. The tunnel was so long they chased the people for twenty-four hours, until the people came out the other end of the tunnel very badly gassed and coughing. . . . The prisoners were brought in to us and I only looked once: four or five of the prisoners were girls between sixteen and twenty. They were nurses and laborers. The girls were brought to us in very bad condition. They were coughing, wheezing and gasping as if they had bad, very bad asthma attacks. I took one look and called the doctor. He gave them all injections and doses of adrenalin. The prisoner compound was nothing but a tent with barbed wire around it. The prisoners were not kept apart according to sex. The prisoners were not given proper bedding. The girls were lying on the ground, which was rather damp, and one girl grew more ill. It was the policy that all prisoners must be interrogated. I kept calling the doctor to say, "Doctor, she has pneumonia. I know because I have had pneumonia." The doctor kept saying, "No, no; she'll get better," and she kept getting worse. She was finally evacuated to Lai Khe, to the Third Brigade, First Division hospital, where she died.

They didn't only leave wounded prisoners without care; American soldiers frequently finished off the wounded at the end of a battle and even deliberately killed prisoners. David Tuck who served in Vietnam in an infantry regiment from January 8, 1966, to February 9, 1967, was a witness to these facts. He told in particular:

38

We were operating in an area near a Special Forces camp. So on that day, I believe it was about 1400 hours, I boarded a Hué helicopter. On this helicopter there was the pilot, the co-pilot, the machine-gunner, myself. There were also two dead American soldiers and two Vietnamese prisoners. While we were in the air, one of the North Vietnamese pointed to one of the United States dead, and started to laugh about it. So the gunner, he saw this and told the pilot about it and the pilot said, "Throw him out." So he picked up the man — the man was tied anyway, bound — and threw him out of the helicopter. . . . So then when we got back to base camp, such a thing is an everyday thing, you know, we didn't think too much of it.

The Tribunal asked the witness if the person responsible for the mission didn't have to make a report on the missing prisoner; the witness answered, "It is true that he would have to write a report saying that one of the prisoners had disappeared. But you could always get around this by saying that the man attempted to escape, and we had to shoot him or that he was suicidal and jumped out of the helicopter."

Even after the interrogation sessions, the torture may be continued. At Camp Holloway, near Pleiku, Tuck saw a prisoner who had just been tortured, locked "in a barbed wire cage in which he was on his hands and knees. And if he made any moves, the barbs pressed into his flesh." He added: "They kept him there for two days." Witness Donald Duncan, Special Forces officer in Vietnam from March, 1964, to September, 1965, confirmed the existence of these cages where, he specified, prisoners are left out in the sun for whole days, without being able to move. The torture often ended with the murder of the prisoner; Duncan watched the disembowelment of a prisoner whose gall bladder was torn out.

The statement of these monstrous practices largely suffices to show how far we are from the Third Geneva Convention. However, that is not all: contrary to the stipulations of this Convention, women and even children are interrogated. Martinsen saw women and adolescents tortured. Lastly, the very places of detention in no way conform to the obligations of the Third Convention. Martinsen gave the following description:

A temporary center is made in general of about thirty barracks surrounded with barbed wire. No beds, no sanitary facilities. Food is scarce, cold. . . . A permanent camp is more extended, with a floor and sanitary facilities. I saw a camp run by the South Vietnamese. I didn't go inside but it looked like a concentration camp. . . . Very often the prisoners complain to the interrogators that the Military Police take their personal effects and money. Sometimes there is embezzlement of money meant for the administration.

Officer Donald Duncan, who in his duties on

the Special Forces staff had precise information on the military situation in Vietnam (he did briefings especially for General Westmoreland and for Secretary McNamara), confirmed that ill treatment, torture and execution of prisoners, far from being isolated cases, happen daily on a large scale. He himself observed or had direct information on analogous facts in seventy-five per cent of Special Forces camps.

THE CIVILIAN POPULATION

1) REPRISALS: Ever since the Geneva Accords and contrary to the provisions of these Accords, the civilian population has always been the object of reprisals. First, individual reprisals. These are numerous and arbitrary: former resisters to French colonialism, parents and friends of resisters or, after 1960, of "Vietcong," those in sympathy with the National Liberation Front or those suspected to be so. These political prisoners are subjected to interrogations accompanied by torture and thrown into prison without a trial; there they undergo "communist re-education courses" and are forced to salute the flag of the Saigon government. Those who resist indoctrination continue to be tortured daily. The others are scarcely better treated. One of the Tribunal's witnesses, Mrs. Pham Thi Yen, a Saigon pharmacist, was arrested as a former resister to French colonialism suspected of subversive activities. She came to trial

on March 25, 1963, before a military court and was condemned for "treason" to hard labor for life. She was in various prisons and tortured in each of them by water, blows and hanging. Her parents were tortured in her presence. In 1966 she was transferred to the prison of Poulo Condor Island where the French had never imprisoned women. She stated:

> I want to point out to you that I was one of the few to appear before a court. Almost all the prisoners were imprisoned without any other form of trial. I found myself with prisoners who had been there, without having been judged, for eight years; they were still at Poulo Condor the day of my liberation. . . . The regime there is very hard. The executioners gave us bleached rice without vegetables to eat. The majority of the prisoners have beriberi, neuritis, scurvy, tuberculosis, or stomach ulcers.

Another witness, Mrs. Nguyen Thi Tho, agriculturist, described the conditions in which she lived for a year in the same prison, in a room made for one person, without light and almost without the possibility of ventilation: "First we were only 4 but then 8 and finally 12 — still in this minuscule cell. There were numerous cases of suffocation. . . ." Water itself has been rationed: less than a cup a day at Poulo Condor and nothing for the toilet. According to these two witnesses who lived there at different times, the purpose of this prison was the extermination of the prisoners. Hundreds of people died there from weakness or ill treatment or epidemic. According to official statistics of the South Vietnamese administration one of these epidemics caused three hundred deaths from July to September, 1957. If we consider that many other prisons have a regime that is very little different, those who die in prison must figure in the thousands. Four hundred thousand persons are still in these South Vietnamese jails, according to reliable sources. Mrs. Pham Thi Yen specified that she and her companions were transported to Poulo Condor in airplanes piloted by Americans and that American delegations came in general each month to "visit" the prisons where she was held but that they never came into the prisoners' quarters nor asked them anything.

As for massive reprisals, this is what is gathered from the information given in the international press and especially in the American press as well as in the testimony to the Tribunal: bombings, followed in South Vietnam by systematic raiding of villages suspected of sheltering "Vietcong" kills thousands upon thousands of inhabitants. American troops then level the raided villages, leaving the survivors no other choice but refugee camps. One witness before the Tribunal, a French reporter who accompanied air-transported American troops on some of their missions, told about the raid of a village thirty kilometers from Saigon:

> The Iroquois, after having dropped their men, climbed very high in the sky. Then they dived in tight rows on the straw huts, launched strings of rockets . . . gained altitude again, dived again in order to shoot at the silhouettes running away from the flaming houses.
>
> Each house was carefully inspected. One could perceive that panic had taken over their inhabitants. Bowls full of rice and chopsticks were left on the tables. . . . In certain homes the water in the pots was still boiling hot.

Numerous witnesses have described similar scenes. Witness Martinsen watched the methodical destruction by bulldozer of one of these villages, Ben Suc. Witness Tuck participated in numerous raids. This is what he said:

> Also it was common practice that if we received any shots from a village to have what we call a "mad minute." This means that for one minute everybody would set loose tanks, machine-guns and everything they had into this village, because that way we had assumed that until proven otherwise, *every Vietnamese was a Vietcong*.

Numerous American sources give the proportion of ten civilian dead for one enemy. Again from an American source, civilian losses in South

44

Vietnam have gone up from 1961 to 1964, to 160,000 dead; from 1964 to 1966, to 415,000 dead. Since the beginning of the war at least 250,000 children have died in Vietnam, 750,000 others have been wounded or permanently mutilated; hundreds of thousands wander homeless or are placed in camps.

Donald Duncan, Special Forces officer, exposed what happened to civilians after the raids:

> First of all, there was no arrest in the proper sense of the word. The people were just forcibly taken away from whatever they were doing and there was an initial interrogation at that point. For example, "Are you a member of the National Liberation Front?" or "Are you a Vietcong?" As you might suspect, not too many people admit to that, under those circumstances. And then the following question would be: "Do you know where they are?" or "Do you know who is?" And more often than not, this is accompanied by violence especially if you are operating in an area of contention or a known National Liberation Front stronghold or controlled area. The people are eventually broken down roughly into the categories of suspected "hard-core VC," sympathizers to the National Liberation Front, or possibly innocent.

During such a sorting, witness David Tuck admits to having struck down a woman by order of a superior, simply because one of her gestures seemed suspicious.

2) DEPORTATION: While "Vietcong" and villagers suspected of being so are led off to camps where they will undergo more intensive interrogation, innocent civilians are taken in trucks to refugee camps, "strategic hamlets" or, more recently, "new life hamlets," three different names designating the same reality, concentration camps. Witness Tuck described a refugee camp:

> The refugee camp is usually located near a Special Forces camp. You have a lot of wooden and tin huts, just thrown together haphazardly. Usually the ground is bare: no vegetation or anything, no trees. And there is also a barbed-wire fence surrounding them and only one entrance. At night the people have to be in before dark, before about 1800 hours anyway.

Vietnamese as well as American witnesses who have lived in Vietnam or stayed there give the same description of these camps before the Tribunal and all add that living conditions — material, sanitary, medical and moral — are deplorable. Duncan said:

> These camps are "garbage pits". . . . The conditions under which these people are forced to live are, by any standards, appalling. There is usually a grave shortage of water, perhaps one water point for two hundred people. In other cases water has to be brought in. They are lucky to have enough water for cooking and drinking, leaving very little for

sanitary purposes. The latrine facilities, if they exist, are of the worst order. There is very little for these people to do, no form of creative work. It's simply a matter of sitting around and letting time pass by. I myself did not see any evidence of physical abuse . . . but there was overcrowding. . . . You could usually smell these camps long before you came to them because of the lack of sanitary facilities.

All the testimony on these camps mentions the fact that a large number of refugees, women or young girls, are forced to turn to prostitution in order to survive.

Duncan spoke the pretended difference between the strategic hamlets and "New Life" hamlets in these terms:

I haven't actually seen the physical displacement of large numbers of people. However, the reports exist in American Headquarters. . . . The strategic hamlets, from the documents I have read . . . were essentially nothing more than concentration camps. The people were forcibly removed. The idea came of course from the British experience in Malaya. The idea was to take the sea away from the fish, to deny the National Liberation Front access to information, supplies, recruiting, etc. In the "New Life" hamlet, theoretically at least, the people are supposed to be given something to do; in other words, it's a new home. . . . The idea, the funding and the

47

supplies come from American forces. The Vietnamese are supposed to do the actual handling of this; in other words, they are the ones physically controlling these camps. More often than not it is the common thing that much of the money, food supplies, clothing, etc., never get to the people. It ends up on the black market. . . . When complaints are made, the Americans say, "Well, the Vietnamese are in charge and we can't interfere."

The Ky government has estimated the population of regroupment camps at 1.8 million (mostly women and children). That is already an enormous figure. However Senator Edward Kennedy declared on October 31, 1967, that in fact approximately one third of the Vietnamese population is displaced. Don Luce, director of the International Voluntary Service, the largest American civilian organization in Vietnam, from 1961 to 1967 (he has since resigned) insists on the fact that the camps, far from having the protection of civilians as a goal, are generally installed in particularly inhospitable or even dangerous places. He states cases where the camps are used for military or strategic purposes; for example refugees are installed around a military headquarters, so that their presence deters the enemy from mortar attacks.

All this testimony, and much more, convinced the International War Crimes Tribunal that the living conditions in these camps and hamlets do not at all correspond to the obligations that civilized nations are supposed to fulfill according to customary law nor to the Fourth Geneva Convention of 1949 which stipulates among other things:

> The Detaining Power is bound to take all necessary and possible measures to ensure that protected persons shall, from the outset of their internment, be accommodated in buildings or quarters which afford every possible safeguard as regards hygiene and health, and provide efficient protection against the rigours of the climate and the effects of the war. In no case shall permanent places of internment be situated in unhealthy areas, or in districts the climate of which is injurious to the internees. . . .

Not only the material conditions are in question: the very existence and purposes of these camps and hamlets are illegal: the fourth Convention, which provides for sanitary and safe zones and localities so as to shelter the wounded, sick, crippled, aged, children under fifteen, pregnant women (Article 14) as well as neutral zones (Article 15), stipulates that these zones can in no case be constituted without the formal accord of the parties in conflict. They must not thus serve American strategy: legally the principle of "strategic hamlets" is anything but valid.

The International War Crimes Tribunal thus judged that the United States is guilty of serious violations of the 1949 Geneva Conventions, in par-

49

ticular Conventions Three and Four, to the detriment of millions of people whose living conditions are similar to those of a concentration camp. The Tribunal concluded that this guilt is augmented by the fact that the United States has signed these four Conventions, and so they are a part of "the Supreme Law of the Land" according to the Constitution.

From Aggression to Genocide

It is easy for the American government which has all the data at hand and which makes all the decisions to foresee that it is the entire Vietnamese population which it threatens with extermination by massive bombings, especially with new weapons, by these inhumane methods forbidden by the laws of war but used daily by American armed forces and their satellites, by these infringements on the life and liberty of people and on the material, familial, social and moral living conditions of a nation. That is why the International War Crimes Tribunal wanted to determine if the totality of these acts, committed within a war of aggression, could be classified as genocide. The legal commission of the Tribunal, in order to answer this question, examined the terms of the International Convention of December 9, 1948, on Genocide, which defines this crime.

Even before the 1948 Convention, the Nuremberg Tribunal had condemned, under the qualification of crimes against humanity, "murder, extermination, enslavement, deportation and other inhuman acts committed against any civilian population before or during war, or persecutions on political, racial or religious grounds . . ." The Nuremberg Tribunal did not use the term genocide in its judgment. But the day after the verdict against Nazi German war criminals, December 11, 1946, The United Nations General Assembly unanimously passed two resolutions. The first confirmed the principles contained in the Charter and judgment of the Tribunal, thus recognizing them as fundamental principles of international law. The second resolution solemnly condemned genocide and instructed the Economic and Social Council to undertake the necessary studies to prepare a convention on genocide. The International Convention on Genocide was signed on December 9, 1948.

Can the United States take refuge in the fact that it didn't ratify this Convention? The International War Crimes Tribunal did not judge thus, for it established that the source of the international condemnation of genocide is not this Convention but the international customary law. The Convention only confirms the international customary law to determine the outlines of the notion of genocide. In this respect, the terms of the preamble of the first article of this Convention are clear:

The Contracting Parties,

Having considered the declaration made by the General Assembly of the United Nations in its resolution 96 dated 11th December, 1946, that genocide is a crime under international law, contrary to the spirit and aims of the United Nations and condemned by the civilized world;

Recognizing that at all periods of history genocide has inflicted great losses on humanity, and

Being convinced that, in order to liberate mankind from such an odious scourge, international co-operation is required:

Hereby agree as hereinafter provided:

Article 1 — The Contracting Parties confirm that genocide, whether committed in time of peace or in time of war, is a crime under international law which they undertake to prevent and to punish.

Article 2 of the Convention defines genocide:

In the present Convention, genocide means any of the following acts committed with intent to destroy, in whole or in part, a national, ethnic, racial, or religious group, as such:

a) Killing members of the group;

b) Causing serious bodily or mental harm to members of the group;

c) Deliberately inflicting on the group conditions of life calculated to bring about its physical destruction in whole or in part;

d) Imposing measures intended to prevent births within the group;

e) Forcibly transferring children of the group to another group.

After its executive president Jean-Paul Sartre had read the following analysis on genocide which constituted the findings* of the Roskilde judgment on this point, the Tribunal unanimously declared the United States guilty of the crime of genocide.

*The members had voted the night before in a private session to unanimously adopt the Sartre text.

On Genocide

BY JEAN-PAUL SARTRE

THE WORD "genocide" is relatively new. It was coined by the jurist Raphael Lemkin between the two world wars. But the fact of genocide is as old as humanity. To this day there has been no society protected by its structure from committing that crime. Every case of genocide is a product of history and bears the stamp of the society which has given birth to it. The one we have before us for judgment is the act of the greatest capitalist power in the world today. It is as such that we must try to analyze it — in other words, as the simultaneous expression of the economic infrastructure of that power, its political objectives and the contradictions of its present situation.

In particular, we must try to understand the genocidal intent in the war which the American government is waging against Vietnam, for Article 2 of the 1948 Geneva Convention defines genocide on the basis of intent; the Convention was tacitly referring to memories which were still fresh.

Hitler had proclaimed it his deliberate intent to exterminate the Jews. He made genocide a political means and did not hide it. A Jew had to be put to death, whoever he was, not for having been caught carrying a weapon or for having joined a resistance movement, but simply *because he was a Jew*. The American government has avoided making such clear statements. It has even claimed that it was answering the call of its allies, the South Vietnamese, who had been attacked by the communists. Is it possible for us, by studying the facts objectively, to discover implicit in them such a genocidal intention? And after such an investigation, can we say that the armed forces of the United States are killing Vietnamese in Vietnam for the simple reason that they are Vietnamese?

This is something which can only be established after an historical examination: the structure of war changes right along with the infrastructures of society. Between 1860 and the present day, the meaning and the objectives of military conflicts have changed profoundly, the final stage of this metamorphosis being precisely the "war of example" which the United States is waging in Vietnam.

In 1856, there was a convention for the protection of the property of neutrals; 1864, Geneva: protection for the wounded; 1899, 1907, The Hague: two conferences which attempted to make rules for war. It is no accident that jurists and governments were multiplying their efforts to "humanize war" on the very eve of the two most frightful massacres that mankind has ever known. Vladimir Dedijer has shown very effectively in his study "On Military Conventions" that the capitalist societies during this same period were giving birth to the monster of total war in which they express their true nature. One may attribute this phenomenon to the following:

1. The competition between industrial nations fighting for new markets produces a permanent antagonism which is expressed in ideology and in practice by what is known as "bourgeois nationalism."

2. The development of industry, which is the source of this hostility, provides the means of resolving it to the advantage of one of the competitors, through the production of more and more *massively* destructive weapons. The consequence of this development is that it becomes increasingly difficult to make any distinction between the front and behind the lines, between the civilian population and the soldiers.

3. At the same time, new military objectives — the factories — arise near the towns. And even when they are not producing material directly for the armies, they maintain, at least to some extent, the economic strength of the country. It is precisely this strength that the enemy aims to destroy: this is at once the aim of war and the means to that end.

4. The consequence of this is that everyone is mobilized: the peasant fights at the front, the worker fights behind the lines, the peasant women take over for their husbands in the fields. This *total* struggle of nation against nation tends to make the worker a soldier too, since in the last analysis the power which is economically stronger is more likely to win.

5. The democratic façade of the bourgeois nations and the emancipation of the working class have led to the participation of the masses in politics. The masses have no control at all over government decisions, but the middle classes imagine that by voting they exercise some kind of remote control. Except in cases of defensive wars, the working classes are torn between their desire for peace and the nationalism which has been instilled in them. Thus war, seen in a new light and distorted by propaganda, becomes the ethical decision of the whole community. All the citizens of each warring nation (or almost all, after they have been manipulated) are the enemies of all those of the other country. War has become absolutely total.

6. These same societies, as they continue their technological expansion, continue to extend the scope of their competition by increasing communications. The famous "One World" of the Americans was already in existence by the end of the nineteenth century when Argentine wheat dealt a final blow to English agriculture. Total war is no longer

only between all members of one national community and all those of another: it is also total because it will very likely set the whole world up in flames.

Thus, war between the bourgeois nations — of which the 1914 war was the first example but which had threatened Europe since 1900 — is not the "invention" of one man or one government, but simply a necessity for those who, since the beginning of the century, have sought to "extend politics by other means." The option is clear: either *no* war or *that* kind of total war. Our fathers fought that kind of war. And the governments who saw it coming, with neither the intelligence nor the courage to stop it, were wasting their time and the jurists' time when they stupidly tried to "humanize" it.

Nevertheless, during the First World War a genocidal intent appeared only sporadically. As in previous centuries, the essential aim was to crush the military power of the enemy and only secondarily to ruin his economy. But even though there was no longer any clear distinction between civilians and soldiers, it was still only rarely (except for a few terrorist raids) that the civilian population was expressly made a target. Moreover, the belligerent nations (or at least those who were doing the fighting) were industrial powers. This made for a certain initial balance: against the possibility of any real extermination each side had its own deterrent force — namely the power of applying the law of "an eye for an eye." This explains why, in the midst of the carnage, a kind of prudence was maintained.

However, since 1830, throughout the last century and continuing to this very day, there have been countless acts of genocide outside Europe. Some were reflections of authoritarian political structures and the others — those which we must understand in order to comprehend the growth of American imperialism and the nature of the Vietnam war — came out of the internal structures of capitalist democracies. To export their products and their capital, the great powers, particularly England and France, set up colonial empires. The name "overseas possessions" given by the French to their conquests indicates clearly that they had been able to acquire them only by wars of aggression. The adversary was sought out in his own territory, in Africa and Asia, in the underdeveloped countries, and far from waging "total war" (which would have required an initial balance of forces), the colonial powers, because of their overwhelming superiority of firepower, found it necessary to commit only an expeditionary force. Victory was easy, at least in conventional military terms. But since this blatant aggression kindled the hatred of the civilian population, and since civilians were potentially rebels and soldiers, the colonial troops maintained their authority by terror — by perpetual massacre. These massacres were genocidal in character: they aimed at the destruction of "a part of an ethnic, national, or religious group" in order to terrorize the remainder and to wrench apart the indigenous society.

After the bloodbath of conquest in Algeria during the last century, the French imposed the *Code Civil,* with its middle-class conceptions of property and inheritance, on a tribal society where each community held land in common. Thus they systematically destroyed the economic infrastructure of the country, and tribes of peasants soon saw their lands fall into the hands of French speculators. Indeed, colonization is not a matter of mere conquest as was the German annexation of Alsace-Lorraine; it is by its very nature an act of cultural genocide. Colonization cannot take place without systematically liquidating all the characteristics of the native society — and simultaneously refusing to integrate the natives into the mother country and denying them access to its advantages. Colonialism is, after all, an economic system: the colony sells its raw materials and agricultural products at a reduced price to the colonizing power. The latter, in return, sells its manufactured goods to the colony at world-market prices. This curious system of trade is only possible if there is a colonial subproletariat which can be forced to work for starvation wages. For the subject people this inevitably means the extinction of their national character, culture, customs, sometimes even language. They live in their underworld of misery like dark phantoms ceaselessly reminded of their sub-humanity.

However, their value as an almost unpaid labor force protects them, to a certain extent, against physical genocide. The Nuremberg Tribunal was still fresh in people's minds when the French massacred forty-five thousand Algerians at Setif, as an "example." But this sort of thing was so commonplace that no one even thought to condemn the French government in the same terms as they did the Nazis.

But this "deliberate destruction of a part of a national group" could not be carried out any more extensively without harming the interests of the French settlers. By exterminating the subproletariat, they would have exterminated themselves as settlers. This explains the contradictory attitude of these *pieds-noirs* during the Algerian war: they urged the Army to commit massacres, and more than one of them dreamed of total genocide. At the same time they attempted to compel the Algerians to "fraternize" with them. It is because France could neither liquidate the Algerian people nor integrate them with the French that it lost the Algerian war.

These observations enable us to understand how the structure of colonial wars underwent a transformation after the end of the Second World War. For it was at about this time that the colonial peoples, enlightened by that conflict and its impact on the "empires," and later by the victory of Mao Tse-tung, resolved to regain their national independence. The characteristics of the struggle were determined from the beginning: the colonialists had the superiority in weapons, the indigenous population the advantage of numbers. Even in Algeria — a colony where there was settlement as much as there was exploitation — the proportion of *colons* to natives was one to nine. During the two world wars, many of the colonial peoples had been trained as soldiers and had become experienced fighters. However, the short supply and poor quality of their arms — at least in the beginning — kept the number of fighting units low. These objective conditions dictated their strategy, too: terrorism, ambushes, harassing the enemy, extreme mobility of the combat groups which had to strike unexpectedly and disappear at once. This was made possible only by the support of the entire population. Hence the famous symbiosis between the liberation forces and the masses of people: the former everywhere organizing agrarian reforms, political organs and education; the latter supporting, feeding and hiding the soldiers of the army of liberation, and replenishing its ranks with their sons.

It is no accident that people's war, with its principles, its strategy, its tactics and its theoreticians, appeared at the very moment that the industrial powers pushed total war to the ultimate by the industrial production of atomic fission. Nor is it any accident that it brought about the destruction of colonialism. The contradiction which led to the victory of the FLN in Algeria was characteristic of that time; people's war sounded the death-knell of conventional warfare at exactly the same moment as the hydrogen bomb. Against partisans supported by the entire population, the colonial armies were helpless. They had only one way of escaping this demoralizing harassment which threatened to culminate in a Dien Bien Phu, and that was to "empty the sea of its water" — i.e., the civilian population. And, in fact, the colonial soldiers soon learned that their most redoubtable foes were the silent, stubborn peasants who, just one kilometer from the scene of the ambush which had wiped out a regiment, knew nothing, had seen nothing. And since it was the unity of an entire people which held the conventional army at bay, the only anti-guerrilla strategy which could work was the destruction of this people, in other words, of civilians, of women and children.

Torture and genocide: that was the answer of the colonial powers to the revolt of the subject peoples. And that answer, as we know, was worthless unless it was thorough and total. The populace — resolute, united by the politicized and fierce partisan army — was no longer to be cowed as in the good old days of colonialism, by an "admonitory" massacre which was supposed to serve "as an example." On the contrary, this only augmented the people's hate. Thus it was no longer a question of intimidating the populace, but rather of physically liquidating it. And since that was not possible without concurrently liquidating the colonial economy and the whole colonial system, the settlers panicked, the colonial powers got tired of pouring men and money into an interminable conflict, the mass of the people in the mother country opposed the continuation of an inhuman war, and the colonies became sovereign states.

There have been cases, however, in which the genocidal response to people's war is not checked by infrastructural contradictions. Then total genocide emerges as the absolute basis of an anti-guerrilla strategy. And under certain conditions it even emerges as the explicit objective — sought either immediately or by degrees. This is precisely what is happening in the Vietnam war. We are dealing here with a new stage in the development of imperialism, a stage usually called neo-colonialism because it is characterized by aggression against a former colony which has already gained its independence, with the aim of subjugating it anew to colonial rule. With the beginning of independence, the neo-colonialists take care to finance a *putsch* or *coup d'état* so that the new heads of state do not represent the interests of the masses but those of a narrow privileged strata, and, consequently, of foreign capital.

67

Ngo Dinh Diem appeared — hand-picked, maintained and armed by the United States. He proclaimed his decision to reject the Geneva Accords and to constitute the Vietnamese territory to the south of the seventeenth parallel as an independent state. What followed was the necessary consequence of these premises: a police force and an army were created to hunt down people who had fought against the French, and who now felt thwarted of their victory, a sentiment which automatically marked them as enemies of the new regime. In short, it was the reign of terror which provoked a new uprising in the South and rekindled the people's war.

Did the United States ever imagine that Diem could nip the revolt in the bud? In any event, they lost no time in sending in experts and then troops, and then they were involved in the conflict up to their necks. And we find once again almost the same pattern of war as the one that Ho Chi Minh fought against the French, except that at first the American government declared that it was only sending its troops out of generosity, to fulfill its obligations to an ally.

That is the outward appearance. But looking deeper, these two successive wars are essentially different in character: the United States, unlike France, has no economic interests in Vietnam. American firms have made some investments, but not so much that they couldn't be sacrificed, if necessary, without troubling the American nation as a whole or really hurting the monopolies. Moreover, since the United States government is not waging the war for reasons of a *directly* economic nature, there is nothing to stop it from ending the war by the ultimate tactic — in other words, by genocide. This is not to say that there is proof that the United States does in fact envision genocide, but simply that nothing prevents the United States from envisaging it.

In fact, according to the Americans themselves, the conflict has two objectives. Just recently, Dean Rusk stated: "We are defending ourselves." It is no longer Diem, the ally whom the Americans are generously helping out: it is the United States itself which is in danger in Saigon. Obviously, this means that the first objective is a military one: to encircle Communist China. Therefore, the United States will not let Southeast Asia escape. It has put its men in power in Thailand, it controls two thirds of Laos and threatens to invade Cambodia. But these conquests will be hollow if it finds itself confronted by a free and unified Vietnam with thirty-two million inhabitants. That is why the military leaders like to talk in terms of "key positions." That is why Dean Rusk says, with unintentional humor, that the armed forces of the United States are fighting in Vietnam "in order to avoid a third world war." Either this phrase is meaningless, or else it must be taken to mean: "in order to *win* this third conflict." In short, the first objective is dictated by the necessity of establishing a Pacific line of defense, something which is necessary only in the context of the general policies of imperialism.

The second objective is an economic one. In October, 1966, General Westmoreland defined it as follows: "We are fighting the war in Vietnam to show that guerrilla warfare does not pay." To show whom? The Vietnamese? That would be very surprising. Must so many human lives and so much money be wasted merely to teach a lesson to a nation of poor peasants thousands of miles from San Francisco? And, in particular, what need was there to attack them, provoke them into fighting and subsequently to go about crushing them, when the big American companies have only negligible interests in Vietnam? Westmoreland's statement, like Rusk's, has to be filled in. The Americans want to show others that guerrilla war does not pay: they want to show all the oppressed and exploited nations that might be tempted to shake off the American yoke by launching a people's war, at first against their own pseudo-governments, the compradors and the army, then against the United States Special Forces, and finally against the GIs. In short, they want to show Latin America first of all, and more generally, all of the Third World. To Che Guevara who said, "We need several Vietnams," the American government answers,

"They will all be crushed the way we are crushing the first."

In other words, this war has above all an admonitory value, as an example for three and perhaps four continents. (After all, Greece is a peasant nation too. A dictatorship has just been set up there; it is good to give the Greeks a warning: submit or face extermination.) This genocidal example is addressed to the whole of humanity. By means of this warning, six per cent of mankind hopes to succeed in controlling the other ninety-four per cent at a reasonably low cost in money and effort. Of course it would be preferable, for propaganda purposes, if the Vietnamese would submit before being exterminated. But it is not certain that the situation wouldn't be clearer if Vietnam *were* wiped off the map. Otherwise someone might think that Vietnam's submission had been attributable to some *avoidable* weakness. But if these peasants do not weaken for an instant, and if the price they pay for their heroism is *inevitable* death, the guerrillas of the future will be all the more discouraged.

At this point in our demonstration, three facts are established: (1) What the United States government wants is to have a base against China and to set an example. (2) The first objective *can* be achieved, without any difficulty (except, of course, for the resistance of the Vietnamese), by wiping out a whole people and imposing the Pax Americana on an uninhabited Vietnam. (3) To achieve the second, the United States *must* carry out, at least in part, this extermination.

The declarations of American statesmen are not as candid as Hitler's were in his day. But candor is not essential to us here. It is enough that the facts speak; the speeches which come with them are believed only by the American people. The rest of the world understands well enough: governments which are the friends of the United States keep silent; the others denounce this genocide. The Americans try to reply that these unproved accusations only show these governments' partiality. "In fact," the American government says, "all we have ever done is to offer the Vietnamese, North and South, the option of ceasing their aggression or being crushed." It is scarcely necessary to mention that this offer is absurd, since it is the Americans who commit the aggression and consequently they are the only ones who can put an end to it. But this absurdity is not undeliberate: the Americans are ingeniously formulating, without appearing to do so, a demand which the Vietnamese cannot satisfy. They do offer an alternative: Declare you are beaten or we will bomb you back to the stone age. But the fact remains that the second term of this alternative is genocide. They have said: "genocide, yes, but *conditional* genocide." Is this juridically valid? Is it even conceivable?

72

If the proposition made any juridical sense at all, the United States government might narrowly escape the accusation of genocide. But the 1948 Convention leaves no such loopholes: an act of genocide, especially if it is carried out over a period of several years, is no less genocide for being blackmail. The perpetrator may declare he will stop if the victim gives in; this is still — without any juridical doubt whatsoever — a genocide. And this is all the more true when, as is the case here, a good part of the group has been annihilated to force the rest to give in.

But let us look at this more closely and examine the nature of the two terms of the alternative. In the South, the choice is the following: villages burned, the populace subjected to massive bombing, livestock shot, vegetation destroyed by defoliants, crops ruined by toxic aerosols, and everywhere indiscriminate shooting, murder, rape and looting. This is genocide in the strictest sense: massive extermination. The other option: what is *it?* What are the Vietnamese people supposed to do to escape this horrible death? Join the armed forces of Saigon or be enclosed in strategic or today's "New Life" hamlets, two names for the same concentration camps?

We know about these camps from numerous witnesses. They are fenced in by barbed wire. Even the most elementary needs are denied: there is malnutrition and a total lack of hygiene. The prisoners are heaped together in small tents or sheds. The social structure is destroyed. Husbands are separated from their wives, mothers from their children; family life, so important to the Vietnamese, no longer exists. As families are split up, the birth rate falls; any possibility of religious or cultural life is suppressed; even work — the work which might permit people to maintain themselves and their families — is refused them. These unfortunate people are not even slaves (slavery did not prevent the Negroes in the United States from developing a rich culture); they are reduced to a living heap of vegetable existence. When, sometimes, a fragmented family group is freed — children with an elder sister or a young mother — it goes to swell the ranks of the subproletariat in the big cities; the elder sister or the mother, with no job and mouths to feed reaches the last stage of her degradation in prostituting herself to the GIs.

The camps I describe are but another kind of genocide, equally condemned by the 1948 Convention:

Causing serious bodily or mental harm to members of the group.
Deliberately inflicting on the group conditions of life calculated to bring about its physical destruction in whole or in part.
Imposing measures intended to prevent births within the group.
Forcibly transferring children of the group to another group.

In other words, it is not true that the choice is between death or submission. For submission, in those circumstances, is submission to genocide. Let us say that a choice must be made between a violent and immediate death and a slow death from mental and physical degradation. Or, if you prefer, *there is no choice at all.*

Is it any different for the North?

One choice is *extermination.* Not just the daily risk of death, but the systematic destruction of the economic base of the country: from the dikes to the factories, nothing will be left standing. Deliberate attacks against civilians and, in particular, the rural population. Systematic destruction of hospitals, schools and places of worship. An all-out campaign to destroy the achievements of twenty years of socialism. The purpose may be only to intimidate the populace. But this can only be achieved by the daily extermination of an ever larger part of the group. So this intimidation itself in its psycho-social consequence is a genocide. Among the children in particular it must be engendering psychological disorders which will for years, if not permanently, "cause serious . . . mental harm."

The other choice is *capitulation.* This means that the North Vietnamese must declare themselves ready to stand by and watch while their country is divided and the Americans impose a direct or indirect dictatorship on their compatriots, in fact on members of their own families from whom the war has separated them. And would this intolerable humiliation bring an end to the war? This is far from certain. The National Liberation Front and the Democratic Republic of Vietnam, although fraternally united, have different strategies and tactics because their war situations are different. If the National Liberation Front continued the struggle, American bombs would go on blasting the Democratic Republic of Vietnam whether it capitulated or not.

If the war were to cease, the United States — according to official statements — would feel very generously inclined to help in the reconstruction of the Democratic Republic of Vietnam, and we know exactly what this means. It means that the United States would destroy, through private investments and conditional loans, the whole economic base of socialism. And this too is genocide. They would be splitting a sovereign country in half, occupying one of the halves by a reign of terror and keeping the other half under control by economic pressure. The "national group" Vietnam would not be physically eliminated, yet it would no longer exist. Economically, politically and culturally it would be suppressed.

In the North as in the South, the choice is only between two types of liquidation: collective death or dismemberment. The American government has had ample opportunity to test the resistance of the

National Liberation Front and the Democratic Republic of Vietnam: by now it knows that only total destruction will be effective. The Front is stronger than ever; North Vietnam is unshakable. For this very reason, the calculated extermination of the Vietnamese people cannot really be intended to make them capitulate. The Americans offer them a *paix des braves* knowing full well that they will not accept it. And this phony alternative hides the true goal of imperialism, which is to reach, step by step, the highest stage of escalation — total genocide.

Of course, the United States government *could have* tried to reach this stage in one jump and wipe out Vietnam in a *Blitzkrieg* against the whole country. But this extermination first required setting up complicated installations — for instances, creating and maintaining air bases in Thailand which would shorten the bombing runs by 3,000 miles.

Meanwhile, the major *purpose* of "escalation" was, and still is, to prepare international opinion for genocide. From this point of view, Americans have succeeded only too well. The repeated and systematic bombings of populated areas of Haiphong and Hanoi, which two years ago would have raised violent protests in Europe, occur today in a climate of general indifference resulting perhaps more from catatonia than from apathy. The tactic has borne its fruit: public opinion now sees escalation as a slowly and continuously increasing pressure to bargain, while in reality it is the preparation of minds for the final genocide. Is such a genocide possible? No. But that is due to the Vietnamese and the Vietnamese alone; to their courage, and to the remarkable efficiency of their organization. As for the United States government, it cannot be absolved of its crime just because its victim has enough intelligence and enough heroism to limit its effects.

We may conclude that in the face of a people's war the characteristic product of our times, the answer to imperialism and the demand for sovereignty of a people conscious of its unity) there are two possible responses: either the aggressor withdraws, he acknowledges that a whole nation confronts him, and he makes peace; or else he recognizes the inefficacy of conventional strategy, and, if he can do so without jeopardizing his interests, he resorts to extermination pure and simple. There is no third alternative, but making peace is still at least *possible*.

But as the armed forces of the United States entrench themselves firmly in Vietnam, as they intensify the bombing and the massacres, as they try to bring Laos under their control, as they plan the invasion of Cambodia, there is less and less doubt that the government of the United States, despite its hypocritical denials, has chosen genocide.

The genocidal intent is implicit in the facts. It is necessarily premeditated. Perhaps in bygone times, in the midst of tribal wars, acts of genocide were perpetrated on the spur of the moment in fits of passion. But the anti-guerrilla genocide which our times have produced requires organization, military bases, a structure of accomplices, budget appropriations. Therefore, its authors must meditate and plan out their act. Does this mean that they are thoroughly conscious of their intentions? It is impossible to decide. We would have to plumb the depths of their consciences — and the Puritan bad faith of Americans works wonders.

There are probably people in the State Department who have become so used to fooling themselves that they still think they are working for the good of the Vietnamese people. However, we may only surmise that there are fewer and fewer of these hypocritical innocents after the recent statements of their spokesmen: "We are defending ourselves; even if the Saigon government begged us, we would not leave Vietnam, etc., etc." At any rate, we don't have to concern ourselves with this psychological hide-and-seek. The truth is apparent *on the battlefield* in the racism of the American soldiers.

This racism — anti-black, anti-Asiatic, anti-Mexican — is a basic American attitude with deep historical roots and which existed, latently and overtly, well before the Vietnamese conflict. One proof of this is that the United States government refused to ratify the Genocide Convention. This doesn't mean that in 1948 the United States intended to exterminate a people; what it does mean — according to the statements of the United States Senate — is that the Convention would conflict with the laws of several states; in other words, the current policymakers enjoy a free hand in Vietnam because their predecessors catered to the anti-black racism of Southern whites. In any case, since 1966, the racism of Yankee soldiers, from Saigon to the seventeenth parallel, has become more and more marked. Young American men use torture (even including the "field telephone treatment"*), they shoot unarmed women for nothing more than target practice, they kick wounded Vietnamese in the genitals, they cut ears off dead men to take home for trophies. Officers are the worst: a general boasted of hunting "VCs" from his helicopter and gunning them down in the rice paddies. Obviously, these were not National Liberation Front soldiers who knew how to defend themselves; they were peasants tending their rice. In the confused minds of the American soldiers, "Vietcong" and "Vietnamese" tend increasingly to blend into one another. They often say themselves, "The only good Vietnamese is a dead Vietnamese," or what amounts to the same thing, "A dead Vietnamese is a Vietcong."

*The portable generator for a field telephone is used as an instrument for interrogation by hitching the two lead wires to the victim's genitals and turning the handle (publisher's note).

For example: south of the seventeenth parallel, peasants prepare to harvest their rice. American soldiers arrive on the scene, set fire to their houses and want to transfer them to a strategic hamlet. The peasants protest. What else can they do, barehanded against these Martians? They say: "The quality of the rice is good; we want to stay to eat our rice." Nothing more. But this is enough to irritate the young Yankees: "It's the Vietcong who put that into your head; they are the ones who have taught you to resist." These soldiers are so misled that they take the feeble protests which their own violence has aroused for "subversive" resistance. At the outset, they were probably disappointed: they came to save Vietnam from "communist aggressors." But they soon had to realize that the Vietnamese did not want them. Their attractive role as liberators changed to that of occupation troops. For the soldiers it was the first glimmering of consciousness: "We are unwanted, we have no business here." But they go no further. They simply tell themselves that a Vietnamese is by definition suspect.

And from the neo-colonialists' point of view, this is true. They vaguely understand that in a people's war, civilians are the only visible enemies. Their frustration turns to hatred of the Vietnamese; racism takes it from there. The soldiers discover with a savage joy that they are there to kill the Vietnamese they had been pretending to save. All of them are potential communists, as proved by the fact that they hate Americans.

Now we can recognize in those dark and misled souls the truth of the Vietnam war: it meets all of Hitler's specifications. Hitler killed the Jews because they were Jews. The armed forces of the United States torture and kill men, women and children in Vietnam merely *because they are Vietnamese*. Whatever lies or euphemisms the government may think up, the spirit of genocide is in the minds of the soldiers. This is their way of living out the genocidal situation into which their government has thrown them. As Peter Martinsen, a twenty-three-year-old student who had "interrogated" prisoners for ten months and could scarcely live with his memories, said: "I am a middle-class American. I look like any other student, yet somehow I am a war criminal." And he was right when he added: "Anyone in my place would have acted as I did." His only mistake was to attribute his degrading crimes to the influence of war *in general*.

No, it is not war in the abstract: it is the greatest power on earth against a poor peasant people. Those who fight it are *living out* the only possible relationship between an overindustrialized country and an underdeveloped country, that is to say, a genocidal relationship implemented through racism — the only relationship, short of picking up and pulling out.

Total war presupposes a certain balance of

forces, a certain reciprocity. Colonial wars were not reciprocal, but the interests of the colonialists limited the scope of genocide. The present genocide, the end result of the unequal development of societies, is total war waged to the limit by one side, without the slightest reciprocity.

The American government is not guilty of inventing modern genocide, or even of having chosen it from other possible and effective measures against guerrilla warfare. It is not guilty, for example, of having preferred genocide for strategic and economic reasons. Indeed, genocide presents itself as the *only possible reaction* to the rising of a whole people against its oppressors.

The American government is guilty of having preferred, and of still preferring, a policy of war and aggression aimed at total genocide to a policy of peace, the only policy which can really replace the former. A policy of peace would necessarily have required a reconsideration of the objectives imposed on that government by the large imperialist companies through the intermediary of their pressure groups. America is guilty of continuing and intensifying the war despite the fact that every day its leaders realize more acutely, from the reports of the military commanders, that the only way to win is "to free Vietnam of all the Vietnamese." The government is guilty — despite the lessons it has been taught by this unique, unbearable experience — of proceeding at every moment a little further along a path which leads it to the point of no return. And it is guilty — according to its own admissions — of consciously carrying out this admonitory war in order to use genocide as a challenge and a threat to all peoples of the world.

We have seen that one of the features of total war has been the growing scope and efficiency of communication. As early as 1914, war could no longer be "localized." It had to spread throughout the whole world. In 1967, this process is being intensified. The ties of the "One World," on which the United States wants to impose its hegemony, have grown tighter and tighter. For this reason, as the American government very well knows, the current genocide is conceived as an answer to people's war and perpetrated in Vietnam not against the Vietnamese alone, but against humanity.

When a peasant falls in his rice paddy, mowed down by a machine gun, every one of us is hit. The Vietnamese fight for all men and the American forces against all. Neither figuratively nor abstractly. And not only because genocide would be a crime universally condemned by international law, but because little by little the whole human race is being subjected to this genocidal blackmail piled on top of atomic blackmail, that is, to absolute, total war. This crime, carried out every day before the eyes of the world, renders all who do not denounce it accomplices of those who commit it, so that we are being degraded today for our future enslavement.

In this sense imperialist genocide can only become more complete. The group which the United States wants to intimidate and terrorize by way of the Vietnamese nation is the human group in its entirety.